Summer at Pine Lake

by Judy Nayer
illustrated by Amy Young

Scott Foresman

Editorial Offices: Glenview, Illinois • New York, New York
Sales Offices: Reading, Massachusetts • Duluth, Georgia
Glenview, Illinois • Carrollton, Texas • Menlo Park, California

Dear Diary,

   Soon it will be summer. The sun will shine. I will ride my bike. I will be out all the time.

       Your friend,

       Mike

Dear Diary,

Summer is here! The pretty flowers are out. Soon we will be at Pine Lake.

Your friend,

Mike

Dear Diary,

We are at Pine Lake! It is very pretty here. I like our cabin.

Your friend,

Mike

Dear Diary,

　　My friend Miles is here too. He smiles all the time. His cat had seven kittens! I like the pretty little one.

　　　　Your friend,
　　　　Mike

Dear Diary,

    We went on a big hike.
We walked a mile! I saw
five little rabbits. I got nine
pine cones.

                Your friend,
                Mike

Dear Diary,

We went to the lake. It was very nice. I got a fish!

Your friend,

Mike

Dear Diary,

    We got a pile of rocks.
We made a fire. We ate my
fish for dinner!

           Your friend,

           Mike

Dear Diary,

    We went to the lake again.
Miles said, "Dive in!" So I did.
The water was nice!

        Your friend,

        Mike

Dear Diary,

　　We went on a hike again. We went up a big hill. It was quite nice up there. I saw a pretty bird.

　　　　　　Your friend,
　　　　　　Mike

Dear Diary,

    We made muffins. We ate them with jelly. Yum!

        Your friend,

        Mike

Dear Diary,

It is time to go. But I'll be back again.

Your friend,

Mike

Phonics for Families: This book gives your child practice in reading words with long *i* as in *pine* and *like*, words with one or two consonants in the middle, such as *cabin* and *muffins*, and the high-frequency words *be*, *friend*, *pretty*, *soon*, and *your*. Read the book with your child. Then have your child read aloud the words he or she finds with the long *i* sound.

Phonics Skills: Long *i* (CVCe); Medial consonants (single and double)

High-Frequency Words: *be, friend, pretty, soon, your*